Adventures in Canadian History

CITY OF GOLD

PIERRE BERTON

The Great Klondike Gold Rush

CITY OF GOLD

ILLUSTRATIONS BY PAUL MC CUSKER

M&S

An M&S Paperback Original from
McClelland & Stewart Inc.
The Canadian Publishers

An M&S Paperback Original from McClelland & Stewart Inc.

First printing November 1992

Canadian Cataloguing in Publication Data

Berton, Pierre, 1920-
City of gold

(Adventures in Canadian history. The great Klondike gold rush)
"An M&S paperback original."
Includes index.
ISBN 0-7710-1445-7

1. Dawson (Yukon) – History – Juvenile literature.   2. Klondike River Valley (Yukon) – Gold discoveries – Juvenile literature.   I. McCusker, Paul.
II. Title.   III. Series: Berton, Pierre, 1920-   . Adventures in Canadian history. The great Klondike gold rush.

FC4047.4.B37 1992   j971.9'1   C92-095069-8
F1095.5.D3B37 1992

Series design by Tania Craan
Cover design by Steven Kenny
Text design by Randolph Rozema
Cover illustration by Scott Cameron
Interior illustrations by Paul McCusker
Maps by James Loates
Editor: Peter Carver

Typesetting by M&S

Printed and bound in Canada

McClelland & Stewart Inc.
The Canadian Publishers
481 University Avenue
Toronto, Ontario
M5G 2E9

Contents

Map appears on page 8

The events in this book actually happened as told here. Nothing has been made up. This is a work of non-fiction and there is archival evidence for every story and, indeed, every remark made in this book.

Adventures in Canadian History

CITY OF GOLD

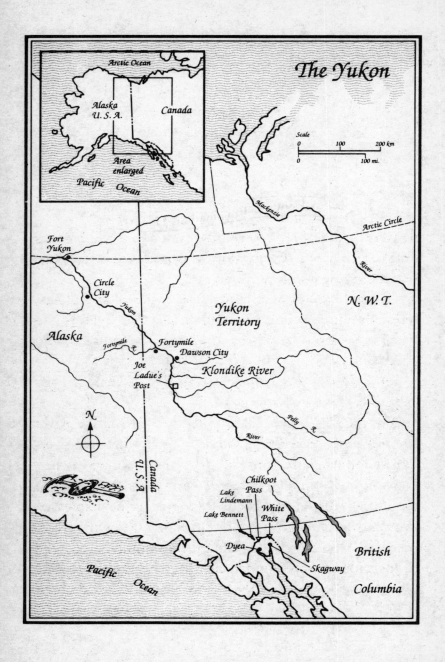

The Yukon

Scale
0   100   200 km
0   100 mi.

Arctic Ocean

Alaska
U.S.A.

Canada

Area
enlarged

Pacific   Ocean

Mackenzie

Arctic Circle

Fort
Yukon

Circle
City

Alaska

Yukon

Fortymile
R.

Fortymile

Dawson City

Joe
Ladue's
Post

Klondike River

Yukon
Territory

N.W.T.

River

Pelly   R.

River

N

Canada
U.S.A

Chilkoot
Pass

Lake
Lindemann

Lake Bennett

White
Pass

Dyea

Skagway

British

Columbia

Pacific   Ocean

CHAPTER ONE

The birth of Dawson

IT WAS THE WORST POSSIBLE site for a city. Who in his right mind would lay out streets and avenues on a flat piece of frozen swamp, so close to the river's edge that the spring floods swept over it?

Covered by a coarse mattress of willows and alders, infested by mosquitoes, a breeding place for typhus and malaria, it would have been avoided by any modern city planner.

But gold camps are not chosen for their setting. They exist solely because of the gold.

And the gold lay just a few miles up the Klondike River from its junction with the Yukon. There, where the rivers joined and where Indians still dried their salmon catches, Dawson was born. Once George Carmack struck it rich on Bonanza Creek on August 16, 1896, it was inevitable that this sprawling wedge of flatland, nestling below the Klondike hills, would become a vibrant community.

Joe Ladue was its founder. He'd been operating a trading post a day's journey up the Yukon when he heard about

Carmack's strike. Joe wasn't interested in looking for gold. He had the most valuable piece of equipment on the river – a sawmill. He rafted it down and laid out the beginnings of a new community.

Joe Ladue knew that dressed lumber would be badly needed – not only for buildings, but also to make the sluice boxes down which the pay dirt is washed to separate it from the heavier gold. That would be the basis of his fortune.

They called the new community Dawson, after Dr. George Dawson, the director of the Geological Survey of Canada. The Americans, who formed nine-tenths of the population, called it "Dawson City," not because of its size, but because it was the centre of a mining district, like Carson City, Virginia City, and Dodge City in the American West, and Circle City in Alaska. The name stuck.

The town began to grow almost immediately, even before it was surveyed. The news of Carmack's strike spread up and down the Yukon like a great stage whisper. Everywhere, men dropped their shovels and headed for Dawson, until the entire river from St. Michael at its mouth on the Bering Sea to its headwaters, 2,200 miles (3,500 km) away in British Columbia, was stripped of men.

They came by boat and raft, drifting down from the headwater lakes or poling upstream from Fortymile and Circle. By early September, 1896, when the birches and aspens were turning the colour of gold, and the buckbrush above the treeline took on a purple hue, the City of Gold came into being.

In its first winter, Dawson City was a tent town, stretched along the margin of the Yukon near the Klondike's mouth. By January there were only five houses in Dawson, one of them belonging to Joe Ladue. The tents, like dirty white sails, were scattered in ragged order between the trees and the frozen swampland.

No one in the outside world yet knew the existence of Dawson, or the gold that nourished it. But as the town grew up around Ladue's sawmill and saloon, a change began to work among those prospectors who for years had had nothing to call their own. The accepted standards of wealth vanished. There was a desperate shortage of almost everything a man needed – from nails to women. There was only one commodity not in short supply – gold. Gold was cheap; it was salt that was expensive – so scarce it was worth its weight in gold.

No other community had a greater percentage of potential millionaires; but its citizens were living under conditions of dreadful squalor. Food became so scarce the most expensive dogs had to be killed because their owners couldn't feed them. Fortunately, a raft load of beef cattle saved the camp from starvation. A Juneau butcher brought the beef into town and sold the lot for sixteen thousand dollars. Within a year he was worth two hundred thousand dollars.

It is important to realize that there were no shops, as we know them, in the Yukon or Alaska at this time. Two trading companies – Alaska Commercial and North American

Trading and Transportation – supplied the miners' needs. Each operated a small steamer on the river – the *Alice* for the A.C. Company, the *Portus B. Weare* for the N.A.T. They carried basic essentials only – flour, tea, and beans, shovels, picks, and wheelbarrows. With more prospectors pouring into the new town of Dawson, that supply could not last.

Dawson operated on the law of supply and demand. It cost one man two hundred dollars just to have the tip of his

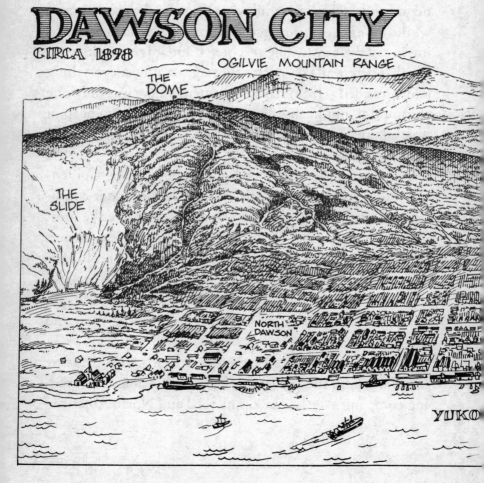

DAWSON CITY

CIRCA 1898

OGILVIE MOUNTAIN RANGE

THE DOME

THE SLIDE

NORTH DAWSON

YUKO

finger amputated. A small keg of bent and blackened nails salvaged from a fire went for eight hundred dollars. There was no writing paper and nothing to read. The only eggs came from two hens owned by a policeman's wife; they cost a dollar apiece. Laundry was so expensive most men wore their shirts as long as possible and then threw them away.

A night on the town, which meant a night in Joe Ladue's saloon, could cost at least fifty dollars. But nobody cared —

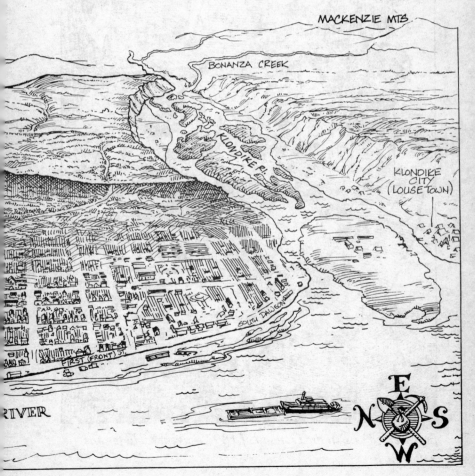

Eggs were so rare in the Dawson of 1897 that they sold for one dollar each.

they could dig it out of the ground whenever they wanted. One man went to work in the morning, came back at night with fourteen hundred dollars in gold. He ordered two whiskies, toasted his former self in the one, making believe his former self was drinking the other, then stuck two cigars in his mouth and smoked them together.

Each man's life was changed by the gold strike. On the day he reached the pay-streak and saw he was rich, he became a different person. Some men could no longer eat or sleep at the thought of mining so much gold. One, who had washed out thirty thousand dollars, became so obsessed by the fear of being robbed that he suffered a mental collapse and shot himself.

Dawson grew slowly all that winter of 1897 as the news spread through Alaska and sifted as far south as Juneau on the Panhandle. All winter long a thin trickle of men had been climbing the Chilkoot Pass. About one thousand men at the headwaters of the Yukon waited for the spring thaw. They hadn't even heard of the Klondike but were heading for an older gold camp – Circle City – in the heart of Alaska.

At noon on May 14 the ice in front of Dawson broke and the whole mass began to move slowly off toward the sea. For two days a solid flow of ice cakes, some the size of houses, drifted past the town. On May 16 the river was open. The first small vessels to arrive belonged to men who had wintered somewhere along the river. The main body of boats was only a few days behind.

The newcomers, sweeping around a bend, came unexpectedly upon two tent cities scattered raggedly along both sides of the Klondike at the point where it joined the Yukon. The first – on the south side – was officially known as Klondike City, but better known as "Lousetown." It was the site of the old Indian salmon camp. On the north bank of the Klondike was Dawson City proper. Within twenty-four hours some two hundred boats had landed with the first news from the outside world.

Soon boats of every size and shape were pouring into Dawson day and night. In Harry Ash's Northern Saloon, the sawdust on the plank floor glittered with fine gold. There was no paper money in Dawson. All business was transacted in gold. When a teenage boy, Monte Snow, walked into the saloon, Ash offered him twenty-five dollars for all the gold he could pan from the sawdust. In two hours young Monte (whose father ran a theatrical troupe) took out $278 in fine dust. It had all sifted out of miners' pokes when they were slapped onto the bar.

By June, Ash was taking in three thousand dollars a day. On the night that he opened his saloon in a permanent log building he took in thirty thousand, perhaps because he had the only piano in Dawson. The previous fall he had written to an old friend in Juneau, Billy Huson, to bring a piano in to Circle City, and all that winter Huson and his wife had been lugging the instrument over the Chilkoot in bits and pieces, the sounding-board carefully wrapped in wool yarn for protection. It was a tiny upright, made in

Hong Kong for the steamer trade, and within a month every dance-hall girl in town had scratched her name on its surface with hatpins. As for the wool yarn, Mrs. Huson knitted it into sweaters, which sold for a handsome profit. Within three months of the opening Ash was able to leave town with one hundred thousand dollars.

By the end of summer there were ten saloons in Dawson, none taking in less than three hundred dollars a night. Some were only tents, others were more substantial. Money meant nothing. Log cabins sold for as much as two hundred dollars a square foot (0.09 sq. m) of floor space. Bacon and tea cost seven to eight times their outside values. Dance-hall girls were paid a hundred dollars a night; town lots were selling for as high as twelve thousand dollars – this at a time when $1.25 a day was the going wage in the outside world for a common labourer.

By summer the population was nearing thirty-five hundred. The ring of hammer and axe was heard all over town. Buildings were sprouting up in helter-skelter fashion. The muddy roadways were covered with chips and sawdust.

Early in June, with the river finally free of ice and the first mosquitoes buzzing over the meltwater in the ponds and sloughs, a shrill whistle galvanized the town into action. A few minutes later the Alaska Commercial Company's little sternwheeler, *Alice,* puffed into shore. The entire populace rushed down to greet her for she was loaded with equal quantities of liquor and food.

The town went on a spree, which continued when, two

days later, the *Portus B. Weare,* owned by the N.A.T. Company, arrived. When these two boats left on the return voyage with their load of wealthy miners, they would carry the news of the great gold strike to the outside world.

CHAPTER TWO

~

Starvation winter

THE NEWS BROKE IN San Francisco and Seattle in late July of 1897, almost a year after the big strike. By August, ships crammed with prospective gold-seekers were heading north from the west coast ports. Only a few hundred managed to get through the passes that fall to reach the City of Gold. As their boats nudged into the fog-shrouded banks amidst cakes of floating ice, the people onshore shouted at them: "There's no grub in Dawson. If you haven't an outfit, for God's sake, turn back!"

Inspector Charles Constantine, the head of the North West Mounted Police, realized that the town was facing starvation. As early as August 11 he had sent a blunt letter to Ottawa saying that "the outlook for grub is not assuring for the number of people here – about four thousand crazy or lazy men. . . ."

The two trading companies began to measure the shortage of food against the new crowds with growing dismay. Both the Arctic Commercial and the Northern American Transportation Company proceeded to give out supplies in small amounts. Prospectors lined up fifty feet (15 m) deep, pleading for a chance to buy, but only one man was allowed in at a time. Each was able to buy a few days' supplies before being sent on his way. A man could have half a million dollars in gold – as many did – and still be able to purchase no more than a few pounds of beans.

As more and more boats drifted in, the air of panic began to settle over the town. Five steamboats were supposed to be heading for Dawson but they hadn't arrived. Where were they? In September, Captain J.E. Hansen, the Alaska Commercial Company's assistant superintendent, headed downstream to find them. He came upon them near Fort Yukon, Alaska, 350 miles (560 km) below Dawson in the shallow and desolate maze of the Yukon flats. All were marooned in low water. Realizing now that Dawson faced famine, Hansen headed back at breakneck speed to warn the town.

On September 26 his canoe was spotted and a cry rippled across the town: "A boat! A boat from the north!" Four thousand men and women streamed down to the waterfront thinking that a steamer with provisions had arrived. As the canoe touched shore and Hansen's tall figure leaped from it, a deadly calm settled over the crowd. He raised his hand in silence and cried out:

"Men of Dawson! There will be no riverboats until spring. . . . I advise all of you who are out of provisions, or who haven't enough to carry you through the winter, to make a dash for the outside. There is no time to lose!"

Captain Hansen warns the people of Dawson that they face famine.

A dreadful silence greeted these words. Most of those on shore had risked everything to reach the Klondike in the first wave. They had won that race, apparently only to lose the prize. Some screamed out their disappointment. One or two actually fainted. Then the mob broke into smaller mobs who threatened to seize the warehouses.

The restaurants closed as the news spread and the miners poured in from the gold creeks. For hundreds there was no sleep that night, as partners pooled what they owned and drew lots to decide who would stay and who would flee. Within a few hours, fifty open boats had pushed off for Fort Yukon. Another hundred were getting ready to leave.

Now those who had been frantic to reach the Klondike were just as frantic to flee. There were desperate scenes on the lower river. At Circle City, Alaska, two of the N.A.T.'s steamboats were subjected to an armed holdup. A committee of six climbed aboard and offered to pay the company's price for enough provisions to last the winter. When they were refused, fifty men with rifles and shotguns emerged from the bushes. They unloaded the cargo, checked it carefully, and paid for it as it was removed. A few days later a second sternwheeler was attacked and was forced to leave the community twenty-five tons (22 tonnes) lighter.

In Dawson, as winter came on, men took to the hills to search for rabbits. Others tried to catch fish through holes chopped in the ice. A few even went into the distant mountains hoping to shoot some big game.

In front of the town, the ice slipped by in a rustling mass.

Then on September 28 to everybody's surprise, the N.A.T. Company's steamboat *Portus B. Weare* puffed into town. John J. Healy, the manager of the Dawson Trading Post, boarded the company's ship and was greeted by Eli Weare, the president. Healy asked how much cargo was on board. Weare replied, proudly, that it was loaded with all the whisky that could be floated across the flats. That drove Healy into a fury, for he had given direct orders to load the boats with food and clothing only. He seized Weare by the throat and almost choked him to death.

Two days later when the second steamboat arrived, also half empty, the Mounted Police realized that a thousand persons would have to be evacuated from the town. With luck they might reach Fort Yukon, where the other steamboats, loaded with provisions, were stranded.

Inspector Constantine posted a notice on Front Street. "Starvation now stares everyone in the face who was hoping and waiting for outside relief. . . ." The Collector of Customs and the Gold Commissioner addressed street-corner meetings urging people to escape. Hansen, of the A.C. Company, ran up and down Front Street from group to group, calling out, "Go! Go! Flee for your lives!" Only Healy remained calm. A tough old frontiersman, he refused to be panicked. He called Hansen a hysterical cheechako (newcomer) and said there was food enough in Dawson for all. "There'll be no starvation," he kept saying. "Some may go hungry, but no one will starve."

In spite of that, he allowed anybody who wanted to take

In the winter of 1897 many of Dawson's homeless spent their nights in McPhee's saloon.

passage on the *Weare* to go to Fort Yukon for a token fifty dollars. Constantine allowed free passage on the *Bella* and five days allowance of food to anybody who would leave town. One hundred and sixty accepted that offer. And so they crowded up the gangplank like defeated soldiers, men who had hoped to become rich by being the early birds in the Klondike. All that fall the exodus continued.

Scores attempted to go back up the frozen river to the passes. As they stumbled on, they threw away their sleds and their food, their clothing and even their shoes. Half a dozen died on this journey. Others returned to Dawson.

The town settled down to its second winter in which poverty, famine, and sickness were fortune's bedfellows. In Bill McPhee's Pioneer Saloon, homeless men slept on benches and tables. But there was gold everywhere – buckskin sacks of it, known as "pokes," stacked like cord wood behind the bar at the Yukon Hotel. Above this glittering horde, the guests were herded into double-decked bunks beneath bare rafters to sleep in their work clothes, with only filthy blankets over them and a nail for a coat-hanger. A crack in the wall served as ventilation, a bit of candle stuck into the logs as light; a red-hot sheet-iron stove supplied an uneven heat.

Gold, which could buy so little, slipped from hand to hand at the gambling tables. One man lost eighteen thousand dollars in a day and a half. Another lost a thousand in five minutes and cheerfully bought liquor and cigars for all.

What would gold buy in Dawson that winter? It would

buy a meal of beans, two apples, bread, and coffee for five dollars in a restaurant before the restaurants closed. It would buy dried potatoes at a dollar a pound, or rancid flour at three. It would buy a one-minute waltz with a girl in a silk dress at a dollar a waltz. One man wanted so badly to dance, he bought seven hundred dollars' worth of dance tickets in advance and danced all week, while a violin scraped and a piano rattled.

Then, on Thanksgiving night, with the temperature at fifty-eight below Fahrenheit (–50°C), a dance-hall girl threw a flaming lamp at a rival, and most of Front Street went up in smoke. Pete McDonald's saloon burned down at a cost of one hundred thousand dollars, but Pete built a new one, aptly named the Phoenix because it rose from the ashes. He had no whisky glasses left because they'd been cornered by speculators who were charging five to ten dollars each for them. He made his own drinking cups of copper and tin, and so the dance whirled on.

CHAPTER THREE

~

The saint of Dawson

THE STARVATION THAT Hansen and Constantine predicted loomed closer. By Christmas, 1897, the stock
of supplies was running low and the last restaurant had
closed its doors. The police were on reduced rations. They
wouldn't arrest anybody unless he brought his own food
with him.

You couldn't escape from Dawson, because the town was
isolated from the world. An occasional dog-driver could be
found who would try to make the trip to Skagway, but the
fee was one thousand dollars, and the passengers had to run
behind the sled, rather than ride on it. Few took advantage
of that.

As the cold came down, the food diminished, the days
shortened, and the sun vanished entirely. The community
slowed to a standstill. Like the hibernating bears, they lay in
their bunks till noon and wolfed their food, half-cooked
and cold.

It cost as much to die as to live. Two men died on
Clarence Berry's claim that winter, and the price of their

funeral was astronomical. It cost two thousand dollars to hire a team of six malemutes to take the bodies into town. The nails for the coffins cost eight dollars and fifty cents a pound (0.45 kg) and the lumber cost forty cents a foot (0.3m). Two workmen took six days to hack the graves out of the frozen ground and were paid two hundred dollars in wages.

By mid-January, flour was so scarce the hunters had to trade an entire mountain sheep to get a sack of it. In April a few hardy souls took advantage of the improving weather to mush in from Dyea and Skagway on the Alaska coast with articles for sale. They didn't bring staples such as flour, meat, or butter, but, with a rare understanding of human nature, brought luxuries. One man arrived with a lady's hat made of black ostrich feathers, which was snapped up at once for $280. Another brought in several tins of oysters and a turkey, ready cooked and dressed. Oyster stew went on sale at fifteen dollars a bowl. The turkey was put on display at the Pioneer Saloon and was raffled off for $174.

As Healy had predicted, no man starved – perhaps because so many had fled the town in the late fall. The real victims were the native peoples. On the Porcupine River north of Fort Yukon, Indian women and children were dying on the trail. Once they had been the best customers of the trading companies. Now they were forgotten.

Hunger's companion was scurvy. The need for a new hospital became apparent, and the man to supply it was Father William Judge, a Jesuit missionary in Alaska. A one-time apprentice in a Baltimore planing mill, he had, for the last dozen years, been a servant of the Lord in the north. He had no interest in gold and no desire for material wealth. An emaciated man with a skull-like face, high cheekbones, and huge cavernous eyes, he looked out at the world from small gold-rimmed glasses.

He had made the long trek to Dawson from Circle City in the fall of 1896, dragging his own sled, which he had loaded with medicine and drugs rather than food. Ill-nourished, he trudged along in harness with his single dog in order to preserve the animal's strength. He knew the new camp would soon be facing plague, and he was determined to build a hospital as swiftly as possible. They called him "the Saint of Dawson."

Since he had arrived he had never ceased working. The task of building a hospital, a church, and a staff residence was enough to tax the energies of a much more powerful man. Yet, in spite of his thin and wasted body, the priest seemed able to perform superhuman tasks. He was his own architect, contractor, and workman. He did every job, including cooking for those who helped him. He roamed the hills collecting dried grasses to fill the mattresses and herbs to amplify his small medical stock. He invented a mixture of muslin, glue, and white lead, which took the place of plaster. He made the furniture himself, using rough boards placed on stumps for pews in his church. He tacked heavy muslin onto frames in place of stained glass windows.

And he suffered bitter disappointments. His church was

scarcely completed after months of careful work before fire destroyed it. Everything was reduced to ashes, including the altar, which he had carved so painstakingly with a common penknife, the hand-hewn furniture, and even the vestments for the choir.

Without complaint he began once again the backbreaking task of rebuilding from the ground up. In this he was aided by a collection taken up by both Protestants and Catholics. Once the church was rebuilt, the priest refused to collect a penny of pew rent or to take up collections at any of his services – a sobering decision in a community where on every other occasion gold was tossed to the winds.

The townspeople helped to raise the thirty-five thousand dollars needed to complete the hospital. Women roamed the mining areas passing the hat. Others held bazaars and dances. In return, Father Judge took into his hospital all who required aid. By March there were forty-five scurvy cases alone, jamming the wards and even the hallways.

Meanwhile, the news of Dawson's starvation winter had seeped out into the outside world. The United States Congress had voted two hundred thousand dollars to buy a reindeer herd, which they believed could be shipped north in time to save Dawson from starvation. The herd of 539 animals was bought in Norway, shipped to New York, then shuttled across the continent by train to Seattle. It was taken north by steamer to Haines Mission at the end of the Dalton Trail on the Lynn Canal. Forty-three Laplanders,

A herd of reindeer, sent to lessen hunger in the Klondike, arrives in Dawson.

ten Finns, and fifteen Norwegians, especially trained for the job, became herdsmen.

In May, 1898, the reindeer finally reached Haines. Nine months later they were still struggling along the trail towards Dawson. By that time the herd had been reduced to a few. They died by the score. Wolves killed some. The Indians shot more. Some strangled in their harnesses. Others collapsed from lack of reindeer moss. By the end the herders themselves were reduced to picking up raw beans spilled on the trail by the gold-seekers.

After a trek of 750 miles (1,200 km), the expedition staggered into Dawson to the amusement of the townspeople. The date by then was January 27, 1899, and the herd was reduced to 114 animals, about one-fifth of its original size. Thus, in that starvation winter, the real victims of starvation had been the wretched reindeer themselves. It was the Klondike Relief Expedition itself that required the most relief.

CHAPTER FOUR

Stampede summer

ALL DURING THE WINTER OF 1897-98, tens of thousands of men and women had been toiling up the passes from Skagway and Dyea at the head of the Lynn Canal. On the other side of the mountain barrier they built more than seven thousand homemade boats. And when the ice finally broke in May, the entire flotilla began the long journey through the headwater lakes and down the Yukon River to the City of Gold.

Dawson was waiting, but for what it did not quite know. A few dog-drivers, who had pierced the winter wall of isolation, brought back exciting tales of an army of gold-seekers camped on the upper lakes. Everyone sensed the stampede was reaching some sort of climax, but no one realized how big it was.

The snow was melting on the mountains at an alarming rate, and frothing little streams were pouring down the sides into the Yukon River. Nature was filling up the river as if with a thousand pumps. Some of the Indians recalled that these flats had been flooded twenty years before and that they had paddled their canoes across the very spot where the new dance halls were being erected. Now everybody realized that Dawson had been built in the wrong place – but how could it have been built elsewhere?

Inspector Constantine walked the riverbank at night, watching the ice stealthily rising, his brow creased with worry. A wave of panic was sweeping across the community. A bad flood could tear this city apart and send horses, tents, dogs, and men hurtling down the ice-choked river.

On May 8, at four a.m., the ice broke with a crackling roar and the river became a hissing mass of floes. Huge grime-encrusted cakes were squeezed out of the channel and flung high onto the shore. As the townspeople watched in horror and fascination, the river crept upward towards the bank. But there was no time for panic because even as the water started to spill into the city, the cry, "Cheechako!" went ringing through the hills. (Cheechako was the native word for "greenhorn"). The first boat had already arrived amid the floating ice.

With the water lapping at their boots, several hundreds trotted along the bank, following the craft for about a mile (1.6 km) before it could be beached. There were five men with dogs and sleds aboard. They had only come from the Stewart River a hundred miles (160 km) away and had no news. The crowd melted away.

Then a second cry went up. A green Peterborough canoe slid in between the ice cakes and again the town rallied. The new arrivals were also old-timers, but they'd actually been at

Lake Bennett earlier that winter and had dragged their canoe down the frozen Yukon until the ice broke.

All during the month of May, while the water rose slowly upon the town, boats in twos and threes slipped in from various wintering points between Bennett and Dawson. But everybody knew the main rush was yet to come. The Mounted Police at Tagish on the upper Yukon had already checked three thousand boats through and more were pouring in every hour.

The early birds made money. Someone brought eggs that were worth as much as gold. Others also brought news: the United States had declared war on Spain! One man arrived with an ancient newspaper soaked in bacon grease. He sold it for fifteen dollars.

More boats trickled in. A man arrived with fifteen hundred pairs of boots and sold them all at fifteen dollars a pair. A man with a load of tinned milk sold it for a dollar a tin. Another made a clear profit of five thousand dollars on women's hats and dresses. One man brought in a scow-load of kittens. He got an ounce (28 g) of gold per kitten from lonely miners craving the companionship of a pet.

A sharp-eyed newspaper editor named Gene Allen arrived in town over the ice, stubbornly determined to be the first to produce a newspaper. He had no printing press but launched it as a bulletin. The *Klondike Nugget* appeared on May 27, typed on a machine borrowed from a correspondent of *The New York Times*. And thus, although the *Midnight Sun* was to be the first to get its printing press into operation, Allen could always say that he had launched the first newspaper in the Klondike.

The following day, May 28, most of Dawson's business section found itself under five feet (1.5 m) of water with cabins near the river already afloat and the townspeople fleeing to the hills. Nobody could move except by boat. But the town didn't float away. The water dropped on June 5, leaving behind an ocean of mud so deep that horses couldn't move through it.

Dawson continued to wait for the great flotilla to arrive

In June 1898 a flotilla of boats poured into Dawson, its passengers keen on finding fortune.

from Lake Bennett. A day passed. Two days passed. No sign yet. And then suddenly, on June 8, the river became alive with boats. They poured in day and night without a break, like a parade, until there was no space along the shore. The boats were tied to each other six feet (1.8 m) deep for nearly two miles (3.2 km) so that Dawson's waterfront looked like a Chinese seaport.

And then the first steamboat arrived from the opposite direction. Five thousand men, women, and children crowded together to welcome her as she puffed into the

bank. "Has she whisky aboard?" came the cry. She had sixteen barrels and it went on sale at once in the bars at a dollar a drink.

Meanwhile a late edition of the Seattle *Post-Intelligencer* had been brought in. A struggle ensued for its ownership. A miner from Hunker Creek got it for fifty dollars and paid a lawyer to read it aloud at the Pioneer's Hall. A crowd followed him down the street as he read them snatches from the headlines. Here was heard the first news of U.S. Admiral George Dewey's victory at Manila over the Spanish fleet in the Spanish-American War. Hundreds cheerfully paid a dollar each to hear that news.

Day after day for more than a month the international parade of boats continued. They brought hay and horses, goats and cattle, kittens and mastiffs, roosters and oxen. They brought sundowners, shantymen, sodbusters and shellbacks, buckaroos and bluenoses, *vaqueros* and *maquereaus,* creoles and Métis, Gaels, Kanakas, Afrikaners and Suvanese.

They brought wife-beaters, lady-killers, betrayed husbands, disbarred lawyers, dance-hall beauties, escaped convicts, remittance men, card-sharps, Salvation Army lasses, ex-buffalo-hunters, scullions, surgeons, ecclesiastics, gunfighters, sob sisters, soldiers of fortune, and Oxford dons.

They brought men seeking gold and men seeking adventure and men seeking power. But more than anything they brought men seeking escape – escape from a nagging wife, or an overpowering mother-in-law, or a bill-collector, or, perhaps, a simple escape from the drabness of the outside world.

And each man brought along a tent. These sprouted everywhere, crowding along the black muck of the waterfront, overflowing across the swamp, spilling into Lousetown, or onto the shoreline opposite Dawson on the west side of the Yukon. They blossomed out on the slopes and hilltops. They straggled by the hundreds along the trails to the gold creeks. From the top of the Midnight Dome above the town, Dawson that spring looked like a field of billowing white – a vast orchard in bloom.

Half a dozen canvas cities had simply been packed up and transferred to the City of Gold. Now sawmills screeched, hammers and saws pounded and rasped, planks and rough timber blocked the roadways, mountains of logs and piles of freshly-sawed lumber grew everywhere. Dawson was a city of sawdust and stumps and the skeletons of fast-rising buildings.

Its main street was a river of mud through which horses, whipped on by their owners, floundered and kicked. In between moved a sluggish stream of humanity, men and women trudging up to their calves in the slime.

Land grew costlier. Building lots fetched as much as forty thousand dollars apiece. The cheapest single room on the far edge of town rented for a hundred dollars a month. In those days a four-room apartment in New York City could have been leased for two years for $120. But an Italian fruit merchant, Signor Gandolfo, paid the same amount for a slender space just five feet (1.5 m) square on the main street. In New York two baskets of tomatoes could be bought for a nickel. At Gandolfo's fruit stand they sold for five dollars a pound (0.4 kg).

The town's character and shape changed daily. Tents, cabins, and men were shifted constantly. Because there were no street addresses it was difficult for new arrivals to find their friends. Those who had spent months in each other's company lost track of one another. Dwelling places with no addresses acquired nicknames such as "the cabin with the screen door," or "the big tent with two stovepipes."

In the crowd of newcomers that summer was hidden at least one murderer, Frank Novak, fleeing from the law. Pressing close behind was a private detective, C.C. Perrin, who had covered twenty-five thousand miles (40,000 km) seeking his man. Now to his surprise, he found himself in the midst of a gold rush.

The chase had been on since February. Novak had gambled away his firm's funds in Chicago and had killed and then cremated a farmer, in the belief the insurance company would think the body was his and pay off Novak's family. But the corpse was identified and Perrin was put on the trail, which zig-zagged back and forth across the continent.

The detective reached Alaska in June and searched among the climbers for his man. The two actually built boats for the river trip within a few miles of one another. At one point Perrin's scow actually passed Novak's without either man realizing it.

In Dawson, Perrin doggedly moved from tent to tent, staring into face after face, searching for his man. One tent made him suspicious; one of its occupants only emerged after dark and kept his hat over his eyes. Perrin pounced and the Mounted Police made the arrest. The detective, who had been six months on the trail, had no interest in seeking gold. Once the prisoner was handcuffed, he made arrangements to leave the City of Gold behind.

By July 1 Dawson had two banks, two newspapers, five churches, and a telephone service. Many made fortunes bringing in papers from the outside world. So great was the hunger for news that bundles of papers were tossed from the upper decks of steamboats before they docked, and the newsboys were able to sell as many as four hundred before the boats tied up. One newsboy was paid fifty-nine dollars in gold for a single paper.

There were now four churches, as well as Father Judge's Roman Catholic building. The Church of England, the Methodist church, the Presbyterian church, and the Salvation Army all opened that summer.

Banks were rising just as swiftly. The Bank of British North America had raced the Bank of Commerce down the Yukon and won. It opened for business in a tent with a rough plank for a counter and an old open trunk as a safe. Here, in careless piles, lay thousands of dollars in currency to be traded for gold dust at sixteen dollars an ounce (28 g). The Canadian Bank of Commerce wasn't far behind. It brought an assay plant over the pass, which allowed it to buy gold dust the moment it opened and to make shipments outside ahead of its rival. Within two weeks it sent three-quarters of a million dollars out of Dawson.

The bank issued one million dollars' worth of paper money brought in over the trail. The words "DAWSON" or "YUKON" were surprinted on each bill in heavy type – a measure taken in case the entire issue should be lost en route. Miners lowered the price on their gold in order to get the less awkward bank-notes. And before long paper currency was circulating.

Everything from gold dust to scraps of paper was used for money. The Bank of Commerce on one occasion cleared a three-dollar cheque made from a six-inch (15 cm) square of spruce plank with a nail driven through it for the convenience of the filing clerk. But the medium of exchange continued to be gold dust.

Most men used a so-called "commercial dust," heavily laced with black sand. It was valued at only eleven dollars an ounce (28 g), and so customers used it to buy groceries or whisky and could reckon that they were saving five dollars an ounce, since the normal price of clean Klondike gold ran around sixteen dollars. On the other hand, bartenders and businesses weighed the dust carelessly, so that a poke worth a hundred dollars was usually empty after seventy dollars' worth of purchases were made. Thus, as often happened in the Klondike, the supposed gain was non-existent.

CHAPTER FIVE

The Klondike carnival

B<small>Y MID-SUMMER</small> Dawson was crawling with people. The largest city west of Winnipeg – and Winnipeg itself was not much larger – Dawson was only slightly smaller than the Pacific northwest cities of Seattle, Tacoma, both in Washington state, and Portland, in Oregon. It dwarfed both Vancouver and Victoria. The Mounted Police put its population at eighteen thousand, with another five thousand prospecting on the creeks. But because gold-seekers were continually arriving, changing their addresses, moving to the hills and then back into town, and pouring off the steamboats, it was hard to guess at the true population at any given moment.

The police figured that more than twenty-eight thousand men had passed the Tagish post on the headwaters of the Yukon. Five thousand of these had stopped on the upper river to prospect. But another five thousand had arrived from other points aboard one of the sixty steamboats that made the trip up the river that summer. The *Klondike Nugget* reckoned that sixty thousand persons would reach the gold-fields before freeze-up, and that would have made Dawson the largest city north of San Francisco and west of Toronto. That was probably an exaggeration. But it's a good guess that well over half that number did reach the Klondike for a few hours, or a few days, or a few months to form part of the jostling crowd that plodded listlessly along the main street.

It was as if the vitality had been drained from these crowds. For the best part of a year they had had their eyes fixed squarely upon the goal. They had put everything into attaining that goal. Now with that goal reached they seemed to lose their bearings. They eddied about in an aimless fashion like a rushing stream that has suddenly been blocked. Thousands didn't even bother to look for gold. All realized, at last, that none had won the great race. The best ground in the Klondike had been staked out by men who were on the spot before the name became known.

Yet none had lost, for there was a strange satisfaction in the simple fact that they had made it. And so they uncoiled like springs that had been wound too tightly, and began to seek out, sheepishly, the former friends with whom they'd quarrelled in the tents during the long months on the trail.

All summer long thousands of aimless men shuffled up and down Front Street still dressed in the faded mackinaws, patched trousers, and high-laced boots of the trail. Their faces, like their clothes, seemed to be the colour of dust. They were like a crowd on a holiday, sightseers at the carnival of the Klondike. Along the boardwalk they trudged, and through the sticky ruts of the roadway, bent slightly forward as if the memories of their packs were hanging heavily upon them.

Behind them, like a hastily built theatrical backdrop, was the line of false-fronted dance halls and gambling-houses, many of them only half finished. A hodge-podge of banners, pennants, signs, and placards, suspended from doors and windows, tacked onto log walls and slung on poles across the street, advertised the presence of a dozen mining exchanges, transport companies, outfitters, information booths, gold dust buyers, dentists, doctors, lawyers, and merchants.

"Gold! Gold! Gold!" the signs read. "Gold dust bought and sold . . . Jewellery . . . Fine diamond work . . . Watches . . . Tintypes . . . Cigars . . . Souvenirs and fine native gold."

At eight in the evening the crowd thickened. The dance-hall callers with megaphones stepped outside and barked out the merits of their wares, as pianos tinkled and fiddles scraped. Inside, silk-clad women danced, liquor flowed over mahogany counters, chips clicked on green felt tables, vaudevillians cracked stale jokes, stock companies staged badly acted dramas, while Projectoscopes and Animatagraphs, the mechanical wonders of the decade, flashed pictures that actually moved on bed-sheet screens, showing U.S. soldiers en route to Manila, or Gentleman Jim Corbett trying to regain his heavyweight boxing title.

Outside on the crowded street in the light dusk of midnight an enormous magic lantern projected advertising messages on the sides of a frame building. Dogs dashed madly up and down through the mud. Newsboys ran through the crowds hawking the *Klondike Nugget*. And from the wharves could be heard the hoarse whistles of steamboats bringing new arrivals.

If by night Dawson was a great carnival, by day it was an enormous bazaar. Thousands who had thrown themselves body and soul into the task of dragging their ton of goods over the mountains and down the rivers were now trying to sell everything in order to get enough money to go home. The wet sand-bar in front of the city was laid out into two streets, known as Wall Street and Broadway Avenue. These were lined with goods selling, for the most part, at half the prices they had fetched in the Pacific coast ports.

After all the shortages there was a glut of merchandise. You could buy almost anything under the sun during that climactic summer. You could buy clothes and furs, moccasins and plug hats, shoes and jewellery, fresh grapes, opera glasses, safety pins, and ice cream. You could buy peanuts and pink lemonade, patent-leather shoes, yellow-jacketed novels, cribbage boards, ostrich feathers, and oxen on the hoof. You could have your palm read, your picture taken, your back massaged, or your teeth filled with nuggets. You could buy Bibles and sets of Shakespeare and pairs of gold-scales by the hundreds, for these had been standard equipment with almost every man. You could buy rifles by the gross at one dollar each; they were worthless in a town where nobody was allowed to pack a gun.

Vegetable and fruit stands, like booths at a county fair, crowded against tents selling dry goods or hardware. Women hawked ice cream made from condensed milk, while others stood perspiring at open bake-ovens rich with the odour of steaming bread. Piles of clothing and piles of provisions lay in heaps in the open, unprotected from the summer rains, while inquisitive men picked at them and bargained, Arab-fashion, with their owners.

Just two years before, this flat had been silent and empty, the domain of Carmack and his Indian friends, the province of the moose and the migrating caribou, the croaking ravens and the spawning salmon. Now for two miles along the river it throbbed and quivered like the aspens on the hillsides.

Once again the law of supply and demand was at work. Few had thought to bring in brooms over the trail: these were now so scarce that they sold for seventeen dollars apiece. The building boom was gobbling up twelve million feet (3.7 million m) of lumber as fast as the twelve sawmills could disgorge it, and nails were selling at almost eight dollars a pound. It cost five dollars to cash a cheque in Dawson and seventeen to call a doctor. Gold-dust weighers were paid twenty dollars a day, and teamsters one hundred. Lawyers made as much as five thousand a month. (In the rest of North America workingmen that year were receiving an average $1.25 a day; union carpenters, about one dollar and a half.)

In July, two wealthy ladies appeared on the scene – the

*The wealthy Mrs. Hitchcock and her companion Miss Van Buren
walk the streets of Dawson.*

first tourists to reach Dawson City. These were Mrs. Mary E. Hitchcock, the widow of a U.S. admiral, and her companion, Miss Edith Van Buren, the niece of the former U.S. President Martin Van Buren (1782-1862). They were in the habit of visiting various points of interest each summer, and this summer, rather than go to Paris or Shanghai, they chose Dawson City. It seemed the most interesting place to go. Of all the thousands who poured into the City of Gold that season, it's probable that these two were the only ones who came merely as sightseers.

They travelled in style – with an incredible cargo. It included two Great Danes, an ice cream freezer, a parrot and several canaries, two cages full of live pigeons, a gramophone, a hundred-pound (45 kg) Criterion music box, a coal-oil stove, a zither, a portable bowling alley, a primitive motion picture projector, a mandolin, several air mattresses and hammocks, and box after box of rare foods: paté and truffles, stuffed olives and oysters. This vast cargo was transported some five thousand miles (8,000 km) by water. Mrs. Hitchcock complained endlessly about the freight charges – they were far more than she'd been used to when crossing the Atlantic.

The strangest item of all was an enormous marquee tent which covered twenty-eight hundred square feet (260 sq. m) and was the largest ever brought into the Yukon. There wasn't any space for it in the main town, so the ladies had it raised on the bank on the far side of the Yukon River where it dominated the landscape. It was so big they found that they had to pitch another smaller tent in one corner in order to stay warm at night.

The two tourists could be seen walking the duckboards of Dawson in their tailored suits, their starched collars, their boater hats, and their silk ties. Sometimes they put on a more picturesque garb – large sombreros, blue serge knickers and rubber boots, with striped jersey sweaters. They wore heavy cartridge belts to which were strapped impossibly big revolvers – apparently in the belief that Dawson was a wild, gun-shooting town like the American western communities they'd read of.

And here on this frozen strip of river bank they acted as if they were in Philadelphia or Washington. One English physician, who had known Miss Van Buren's father, wanted to call but had to send a card saying he couldn't do so because he couldn't find a starched shirt. She graciously accepted this excuse and received him anyway in his serge suit.

The Salvation Army had sent a troop to Dawson and asked the ladies if they could use the marquee for the Sunday service. The ladies were happy to oblige. The following Sunday as the voices were raised in prayer it was noticed that the pigeons had escaped from their cages and were fluttering above the heads of the congregation. One of them finally perched on the music box which mechanically responded with "Nearer My God to Thee." At that the entire congregation rose and repeated the grand old hymn.

Mrs. Hitchcock and Miss Van Buren stayed for the

summer and then took passage upriver in a tiny little steamer, *Flora*. They were shocked by the primitive cabin. There was only one foot (0.3 m) of space to turn around in between the double bunks in the wall. It was quite impractical to undress, except for the removal of an overcoat. There was nowhere to wash, except for a bucket with a rope attached to it which they had to lower over the side into the muddy river. As the boat departed, the two outraged women were heard complaining shrilly about these arrangements. It certainly wasn't what they had been used to.

~

CHAPTER SIX

The "San Francisco of the North"

Hollywood movies have depicted the Klondike as lawless and gun-happy. Nothing could be farther from the truth. Thanks to the presence of the North West Mounted Police, not a single murder took place in Dawson City in 1898. There was very little major theft. You could leave your cabin or tent wide open and go off on a six-week trip and return to find everything intact. A New Zealander named James Dalziel used to go away for a month at a time, leaving his cabin unlocked and his best suit hanging on the wall for all to see. There was a solid-gold watch in a solid-gold case with a massive gold chain in his vest pocket. It was never touched.

The nearest thing to mayhem occurred when Coatless Curly Munro had a quarrel with his wife. Both reached for revolvers, which they kept under their pillows, then took one look at each other, and fled the premises by different doors. (Coatless Curly was a man who believed in such melodramatic gestures. It was his habit never to wear an outer jacket, but to go about in vest and shirt sleeves even in the coldest weather. It was generally agreed, however, that he wore three suits of heavy underwear beneath his outer clothing.)

Nobody could carry a gun in Dawson without a licence, and few licences were issued. One western badman from Dodge City was ejected from a saloon by a Mounted Police constable for talking too loudly. He left like a lamb. The Mountie discovered he was carrying a gun and asked him to hand it over.

"No one as yet has taken a gun away from me," snarled the badman.

"Well," the policeman said mildly, "I'm taking it," and he did without a murmur from his opponent.

So many revolvers were confiscated in Dawson in 1898 they were auctioned off by the police for as little as a dollar and bought as souvenirs to keep on the mantelpiece. The chief crimes were mild ones, such as non-payment of wages, dog stealing, operating unsanitary premises, fraud, unlawfully practising medicine, disturbing the peace, deserting employment, and "using vile language." There were 650 arrests made in the Yukon in 1898, most of them for misdemeanours of that kind. Only 150 were for more serious offences.

To the newcomers the police often seemed superhuman. There was something miraculous, for instance, about the ability of Inspector W.H. Scarth to work cheerfully in below-zero weather without ever wearing mitts or gloves – and without ever seeming to freeze a finger.

When Superintendent Samuel B. Steele took over command from Inspector Constantine that summer his reputation had come ahead of him. He had treated the stampede down the Yukon as he would an army manoeuvre, forcing each boat to check in at police posts along the way, in order to keep track of every would-be prospector. He ruled Dawson with the same firm hand.

There were only two punishments. A culprit was either given a "blue ticket" to leave town or was sentenced to hard labour on the government woodpile. The blue ticket was a serious penalty, especially for gamblers and saloon-keepers, because it meant they could no longer do business legally. The woodpile kept more than fifty prisoners busy at all times. The police and government offices alone used enough fuel to make a pile two miles (3.2 km) long and four feet (1.2 m) square. All of it had to be sawed into stove lengths.

Steele allowed the gambling halls, saloons, and dance pavilions to run wide open, but he wouldn't allow disorderly conduct, obscenity, or cheating. He told the saloon-keepers if he heard of any complaints of unfair gambling he would close them up. He didn't interfere with the liquor traffic – 120,000 gallons (545,500 l) came into Dawson during that season. But he did not allow drinks to be sold to people under the age of twenty-one, nor did he allow children to be employed in the saloons. If a man made an obscene or disloyal remark in the theatre, that theatre was fined and could be closed.

NWMP Superintendent Sam Steele maintained the law with a firm hand.

To the free-wheeling Americans, Dawson's Sunday was remarkable. On that day the town went dead. Everything was closed – saloons, dance halls, theatres, and business houses. They were shut one minute before midnight on Saturday and stayed shut until two o'clock Monday morning.

In order to get around the blue laws some of the theatres began "sacred concerts" at which a collection was taken. A series of "living pictures" of various religious scenes were staged, with scantily dressed performers. The climax was reached on a certain Sunday evening when the curtains parted to reveal a dance-hall queen named Caprice attired only in pink tights and slippers and clinging suggestively to an enormous cross.

Another plan in the summer was the Sunday excursion. The American border was only about fifty miles (80 km) away, and so a boatload of holidayers could easily be transported into Alaska beyond the reach of the Mounted Police. There, on one memorable occasion, some 368 people – gamblers, dance-hall girls, and theatre men – climbed aboard the *Bonanza King* while another hundred embarked on the *Tyrrell*. One boat ran out of fuel and the other developed engine trouble. Both pleasure ships drifted helplessly downstream into the heart of Alaska until all the liquor was drunk. That Monday Dawson remained a dead town since the liveliest members of its population had gone. Theatres, dance halls, saloons, and gambling houses had to stay closed.

When the two steamers finally limped back upstream

and came into sight, the town rushed to the wharf to wel-come the returnees. Steamers' whistles blew wide open and every dog howled in chorus, as several thousand people cheered the girls in their rumpled dresses walking unsteadily down the gangplank.

But the Sunday laws were not relaxed. No work of any kind was allowed on the Lord's Day. One man was arrested for fishing on the Sabbath, another for sawing his own wood. In August, 1898, two men were each fined two dol-lars and three dollars costs just for examining their fishing nets on a Sunday.

On one Sunday a race was arranged between two famous dog teams. The scene along the Klondike valley road was colourful. In the glittering spring sunlight, scores of dance-hall girls and actresses with their hair piled high on their heads, dressed in their finest be-ribboned silks, lined the course arm in arm with saloon-keepers and gamblers in hard hats, stiff collars and diamond studs. Cheers rang out as the two teams came bolting down the hard-packed road – and then raced neck and neck into the arms of the waiting police, who arrested all and sundry on a charge of offending against the Sabbath.

This was Dawson's climactic year. It was a major metrop-olis for exactly twelve months: from July, 1898, to July, 1899. Before that period it had only been an overgrown frontier community with shacks and tents. Afterward it subsided slowly into a ghost town. But for one glorious winter it was "the San Francisco of the north."

Even though it lay four thousand miles (6,400 km) from

civilization and was the only settlement of any size in a wilderness area of hundreds of thousand square miles, Dawson was livelier, richer, and better equipped than many larger Canadian and American communities. It had a telephone service, running water, steam heat, and electricity. It had dozens of hotels, many of them more luxurious than those on the Pacific coast. It had motion picture theatres operating at a time when the projected motion picture was only three years old. It had restaurants where string orchestras played for men in tail coats who drank expensive wines. It had fashions from Paris. It had dramatic societies, church choirs, glee clubs, and vaudeville companies. It had three hospitals, seventy physicians and uncounted platoons of lawyers. Above all, it had people.

None of these citizens was ordinary. Almost every one knew how to build his own boat or his own cabin out of green lumber, how to handle a dog team on a narrow trail, how to treat scurvy with spruce-bark tea, how to carry a pack on a tumpline, and how to navigate fast water. Some had more individual accomplishments: there were gamblers ready to bet fifty thousand dollars on the turn of a card and dance-hall girls who could be purchased for their weight in gold.

They came from all over the world and from every background. And there were scores of newspaper correspondents to report on what they did.

A good number of the newcomers came from the American "wild west." Buckskin Frank Leslie, a famous gunman from Arizona, joined the gold rush. So did Calamity Jane, the camp follower from Deadwood. Irish Nellie Cashman, "the miners' angel," ran a boarding house in Dawson, just as she once had in Tombstone.

For these people there was nowhere else in the world to go. They'd spent all their lives on the frontier, in towns with names like Deadwood, Tucson, and Cheyenne. The west was no longer wild. The frontier had moved three thousand miles (4,800 km) away. And so they walked the streets of the golden city, many clinging to their fringed gauntlets, and their hide vests, and their broad-brimmed hats.

Captain Jack Crawford, the "poet scout" of the west, turned up with his white goatee, buckskin shirt, long silken hair, and scout's hat. He had fought the Indians in the border wars, hobnobbed with Buffalo Bill Cody and Wild Bill Hickok, and served a stint as a U.S. marshal. Now from a hovel known as The Wigwam, he sold everything from hay to ice cream when he wasn't entertaining by composing a poem about anything or anybody on the spot.

One towering figure on the street seemed to have stepped straight out of a wild west show. This was Arizona Charlie Meadows, a former rodeo king who conceived the idea of producing a souvenir newspaper that would glorify the wealthy miners. He raised fifty thousand dollars from that scheme and by the winter of 1898-99 was hard at work planning the Palace Grand dance hall and theatre, which, he promised, would be the most lavish place of its kind in the north.

Dawson was a town of nicknames. Half the community, it seemed, went under such pseudonyms as Limejuice Lil, Spanish Dolores, Deep-Hole Johnson, Billy the Horse, Cassiar Jim, and Two-Step Louie. There was Spare-rib Jimmy Mackinson, so thin that his landlady was said to have refused him sheets for fear he'd tear them with his bones; and Waterfront Brown, the debt collector who haunted the riverbank in order to capture fleeing defaulters; and Phantom Archibald, who spent twenty-five thousand dollars in gold on a colossal binge and thought himself pursued by a long, black python. Last, as well as least, was that curious little creature known as the Evaporated Kid because he was so small that "he looked like a bottle with hips."

Yet in spite of this apparent diversity, the mix of humanity seemed to belong together. Although they had come to the Klondike from every corner of the globe, and although their backgrounds were entirely dissimilar, they had one thing in common: they were there. Others had given up the struggle and retreated; but each of these desperate citizens had succeeded in what he set out to do.

CHAPTER SEVEN
～
Dance Hall Row

Although dawson covered several square miles, spilled across two rivers, and was squeezed up the sides of the surrounding hills, its pulse beat swiftest in those three or four short blocks of Front Street where the saloons, dance halls, and gaming houses were crowded together.

This was the most unstable as well the liveliest section of town. Here the buildings were continually burning down, being rebuilt, changing ownership, being lost and won in gambling games, sometimes changing both their name and their location, so that the street was seldom the same from month to month.

And yet in another sense it never changed, for anyone who walked inside one building might have been said to have walked inside them all. The outside façade was deceptive. The carved scroll work, the ornate bay windows and balconies, the elaborate cornices and pillars were as false as the square fronts that hid the dingy, gabled log building behind.

Though Hollywood films have presented the dance halls

of Dawson with Parisian splendour, the real ones were cheaper and shabbier, and so were the girls who danced within. Like the furniture, they had to be brought in over the mountains and so were plain, sturdy and serviceable – husky women able to withstand the journey.

The interiors were all the same. Most followed the design of the Monte Carlo, a hastily erected two-storey building with large, plate-glass windows facing the street. On entering, the newcomer found himself in a small, rather dark room dominated by a sheet-iron stove with a long, polished bar to his left. Behind it, the bartenders in starched shirts and aprons with white waistcoats and diamond stick-pins stood reflected in the long mirrors at the back.

Beyond this saloon was a smaller room where faro, poker, dice, and roulette were played day and night. Behind that room was the theatre. It consisted of a ground floor with movable benches, a balcony of three rows, with six boxes, and a small curtained stage.

This layout differed only in detail up and down the street. A sign on the balcony of the Opera House reminded customers that "gentlemen in private boxes are expected to order refreshments." It was a mark of wealth for a man to be seen in an opera box surrounded by dance-hall girls, drinking champagne at sixty dollars a quart (1.3 l).

This was one of the great outward signs of success in the Klondike. It showed that these men had won a hand in the hard game of life. The private box in the Dawson dance hall became a sort of symbol. Suspended above the masses on

Gambling houses ran day and night in Dawson.

the floor below, a miner, flush with gold, could feel that he had indeed risen in the world. In the Monte Carlo one night a man who had struck it rich ordered seventeen hundred dollars' worth of champagne to his box.

To many the dance hall was a supreme symbol of achievement. Some men wanted to own one and invested all their gold in a palace of pleasure – not always to their profit. When Charlie Kimball built the Pavilion it cost him one hundred thousand dollars – everything he had. On opening night he took in twelve thousand and was so delighted by this new way of mining gold that he began to celebrate. In one three-month bender, he spent three hundred thousand dollars. When he sobered up he'd lost everything. But for one brief whirl he had been Somebody.

The bar in the gambling houses ran day and night except on Sunday. The dance hall became alive about eight in the evening and ran till six or seven the following morning. The actual dancing, however, didn't really begin till after midnight. Before that there were lengthy entertainments: a drama first, followed by a series of vaudeville acts.

Many a serious drama found its way to the Dawson stages – everything from *East Lynne* to *Camille*. Sometimes invention was necessary. In *Uncle Tom's Cabin* the bloodhounds were represented by a single howling malemute puppy hauled across the stage by invisible wires. Newspapers were used to imitate ice floes. But the critics praised the realistic performance of the actress. It was obvious she really had seen people making their way across floating ice.

Arizona Charlie ran a full-blown production of *Camille*

at his Palace Grand. He had built the theatre by buying and wrecking two steamboats. To open it he held a banquet for forty persons and laid a hundred-dollar bank note on each plate. But the stage production was not entirely successful, owing to a serious piece of miscasting. There was obviously no love lost between Armand Duval, the hero of the piece, and his consumptive lady. It appeared that the man playing Duval was the divorced husband of the dance-hall girl playing Camille. She hated him so much she couldn't bear to speak with him off-stage. At the end of each performance she was in a state of nervous prostration from being forced to make love to him on the stage.

When such entertainments failed, Arizona Charlie could rely on his shooting skills. Dressed in his familiar buckskin, with his black locks hanging to his shoulders, the old scout presented a commanding figure. From his position at the far end of the stage he would shoot glass balls from beneath the thumb and forefinger of his pretty, blonde wife. One night he missed and nicked her thumb. From then on there were no more shooting exhibitions.

The stage shows in the Dawson theatres brought enthusiastic crowds to Front Street because the town was starved for entertainment. Young Monte Snow and his sister once picked up 142 dollars thrown at them as they danced and sang on stage. Little Margie Newman, a nine-year-old child known as the "Princess of the Klondike," sometimes stood heel-deep in the nuggets after she performed a sentimental song.

In the gaming rooms the gold never stopped circulating.

The entire stampede had been an enormous gamble. When the rush reached its height, men were ready to make any kind of wager for any kind of reason. Two old-timers once bet ten thousand dollars on the accuracy with which they could spit at a crack in the wall.

In the gaming-room at the Northern one night in the fall of '98, a neatly dressed man with clean-cut features thoughtfully sauntered over to the roulette wheel and laid a thousand-dollar bill on the red. The black came up. He laid a second on the red. Again the black came up. He laid a third and lost again. Ten times he laid a thousand dollars on the green baize table and ten times he lost. He showed no emotion but strolled over to the bar and asked for a drink. "I went broke," he told the bartender. He gulped down the whisky, turned about, threw a single fleeting glance at the wheel, walked into the street, and shot himself.

Silent Sam Bonnifield was the best known gambler in Dawson. His Bank Saloon and Gambling House, at the corner of Front and King across from the Alaska Commercial store, was the most celebrated establishment of its kind in the Klondike. He was a handsome, quiet man in his early thirties, tall and slender, with eyes of a peculiar unfading blue, who never cracked a smile or uttered a word as he pulled in bets of five hundred dollars at the roulette or faro tables.

He once lost seventy-two thousand dollars as well as his gambling establishment in a poker game. At the eleventh hour a friend arrived and loaned him enough to keep going.

Within six hours Bonnifield had won it all back and cleaned out the customer.

Bonnifield came north with another bold gambler named Louis Golden, better known in the north as Goldie. They ran rival establishments but closed up once a week and played at each other's tables until one of them went broke.

These two took part in the biggest poker game ever recorded in the Klondike. There was fifty thousand dollars in the pot when Goldie raised it by twenty-five thousand. Bonnifield called him and raised again bringing the pot to a hundred and fifty thousand. Goldie triumphantly laid down four queens. Bonnifield, without a word or change of expression, turned his hand over to show four kings and raked in a fortune.

Harry Woolrich from Montana had the distinction of having won and lost fifty thousand dollars in a game in Butte, Montana. He often played for days on end, taking his meals at the table. In Dawson he ran the gambling concession at the Monte Carlo. One night he cleaned up sixty thousand dollars, and determined to give up gambling forever, leave the Klondike, and settle down.

He boarded a parting steamer to the cheers of a crowd of friends who came down to see him off. Alas for him, the boat was delayed. Woolrich went back to the gaming tables and with a magnificent gesture, pulled a half-dollar from his pocket, flung it on the counter, and cried: "Here's my farewell to gambling, boys; I'm through!" He lost the half-dollar, so matched it with another half. He lost again. Twenty-four hours later he was still in the same spot. The boat was long gone. When his money ran out he pulled out the steamer ticket and flung it on the table and lost that, too.

Gambling was the chief amusement in the winter of '98-'99. When a big game was underway, hundreds and sometimes thousands arrived to watch the excitement. If a player had a streak of luck, others would make minor fortunes laying side bets. On one memorable evening, One-Eyed Riley, the night watchman for a navigation company, started a winning streak. Up to this point he had always lost and was always broke. But now hundreds followed him around as he moved up and down the street from table to table and saloon to saloon.

When Riley started to win he forgot about his job and stayed at the tables until morning. By then his winnings were in the thousands. He left Bonnifield's to get something to eat with the crowds following him. Whatever the limit was he played it and won, and moved on. His last stop was the Monte Carlo. Now it was well into morning but his luck still held. Dealer after dealer was used against him to try and buck his winning streak – without success. A mystic aura seemed to surround him. Scores profited by following his bets with money of their own.

In a last-ditch attempt to stop him, the management recruited a card wizard to deal with him. At that Riley finally called it quits. By then he had piled up twenty-eight thousand dollars and was determined to get out of town as quickly as possible before he lost it all again. He was in such a hurry he didn't even bother to collect his wages. It was midwinter and hard to leave Dawson, but he paid a dog-driver a thousand dollars to rush him out over the winter trail.

When he reached Skagway, somebody talked him into a dice game. Riley, flushed with success, lost his fortune in three straight passes.

CHAPTER EIGHT

Death of a saint

Aʟʟ ᴛʜɪs ᴛɪᴍᴇ, while the carnival ran day and night on Front Street, Father William Judge quietly toiled away at his hospital. All the previous summer the steaming swamp on which the town was built, rank with undisposed-of sewage, had spread typhoid, malaria, and dysentery among the stampeders. They jammed every available cot in the hospital, filling the very hallways and crowding Father Judge himself out of his own tiny bedroom.

The priest had one quality in common with all who descended upon the Klondike: he was a believer in miracles. For him the miracles always seemed to come true. It was his practice never to turn a patient away, and one afternoon he accepted twenty more than he had bedding for; but the miracle came. At nightfall three bales of blankets arrived mysteriously on an unidentified sled and were dumped at the door.

Again, early in the fall, he had so many patients that he was forced to put some of them in the upper rooms, which weren't finished because the roof hadn't been completed. As if in answer to his prayers, the storm ceased and there was clear weather for three weeks until the last board was in place.

During the winter he found he couldn't hire workmen to dig a grave in the frozen ground for one of his dead patients. He struggled himself with a pick and shovel until he was about to give up in despair. Out of the gloom two husky miners appeared, told him that they'd heard they were wanted at the hospital, and proceeded at once to complete the grave and cover the coffin.

Father Judge was the conscience of Dawson. Men watched him at his work and felt a little better that they belonged to the human race. It was as if his own example cleansed them of their sins. His little office, which contained nothing more than a narrow bed made of boards, two blue blankets, and a rough wooden drawer in which he kept all his possessions, had long since been turned over to the sick. When he slept at all, he slept curled up in the hallways or in a corner by the stairs. His nurses pleaded with him to take more rest, but he said that only when his work was finished would he have time to sleep.

He rose at five in the morning to hear Mass and to eat a tiny breakfast, frequently sharing his food with others. He did not quit until eleven at night. He always insisted that he be awakened if any patient asked to see him. All through the dark hours he could be seen moving quietly, like a guardian shade, through the wards.

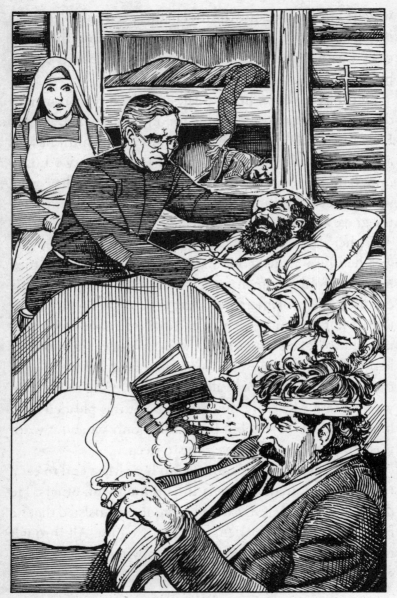

Father William Judge, "the Saint of Dawson."

Judge rarely smiled, yet his face was forever radiant, beaming with what one man called, "an indescribable delight." Despite his frailty he moved with catlike speed; he did not walk upstairs, but always ran.

It would have horrified him to know his hospital was a hotbed of graft. Many of the male nurses waited for a man to die so they could steal his money. It was customary to prescribe a bottle of brandy or whisky for a patient recovering from typhoid, but the attendants drank most of that.

All that fall the feeling grew that something should be done for Father Judge. In spite of heavy donations the hospital was still in debt and so the people of Dawson proposed to pay it off as a Christmas present. A benefit was planned and, although December 25 was the best paying night of the year, Joe Cooper offered his Tivoli Theatre free of charge for the affair.

As Judge's only garment in all those months in Dawson had been a tattered black cassock, patched and worn, it was decided he must have a new suit of clothes for Christmas. A tailor was sent to measure him, but the priest politely refused. The tailor was told to make the suit anyway, together with a sealskin coat, cap and gloves. A presentation was made a few days before the show. But Judge, though moved, explained he could not, as a Jesuit, own anything. The presentation committee urged the clothing upon him, pointing out that most of the donors were Protestants. In the end he relented.

He was reluctant to attend the minstrel show in his

honour, but they talked him into it. When George Noble, the master of ceremonies, rose to make a little speech referring to him as the "grand old man of Dawson," the audience went wild. He was taken up on the stage against his wishes and the cheering continued for five minutes, but this was the only time he appeared in his new clothes. The following day he was seen again in his threadbare robes.

His time was running out and the whole town knew it. Although he was only forty-five years old, he looked closer to seventy. Overwork had lowered his resistance. Two weeks before Christmas the word spread across the community that he was ill with pneumonia. A pall settled over Dawson. As if to accentuate the mood, the temperature dropped to 50° below Fahrenheit ($-46°C$). The snow turned dry as sand, and the smoke from the buildings rose vertically into the still air to hang over the river valley in a pale shroud.

It seemed as if the whole community was slowing to a dead stop. It was so cold the horses couldn't be worked. After a few days there was scarcely any life in the streets. Moving slowly, like ungainly animals, to protect their lungs, bundled in furs to their very ears, men made brief forays into the cold and then retreated again into the steaming interiors. Windows froze in solid, while cabins even a few yards distant were blurred by the fog that smothered the community.

In the hospital on the hill the death watch began as Judge clung precariously to life. He sank lower day by day. Hundreds of inquiries poured in asking how he was, while gifts arrived daily, including a case of champagne worth thirty dollars a pint. A wealthy prospector, Skiff Mitchell, made his way to Judge's bedside. He was an old friend of the priest, although a Protestant, and when he saw the wasted figure on the couch, the tears rolled down his cheeks.

"Why are you crying?" Judge asked him. "We have been old friends almost since I came into the country."

"We can't afford to lose old friends like you," Mitchell replied.

"You've got what you came for," the priest reminded him. "I too have been working for a reward. Would you keep me from it?"

He seemed anxious to die. When the nuns said they would pray hard for him to stay alive, he answered quite cheerfully: "You may do what you please, but I am going to die."

The end came on January 16. Dawson went into deep mourning. "If the whole town had slipped down the river, it would not have been more of a shock," someone wrote later. Shops and dance halls closed their doors and even the houses were draped in black.

It took two and a half days to hack the dead priest's grave out of the hard, frozen soil, but there was no shortage of men for the task. When the body was taken to its rest, the grieving population followed. Nothing would do but that the casket cost one thousand dollars and be made of the finest material. It was a gesture in keeping with the general ostentation of the community, though the shrivelled figure within would have shuddered at the thought.

CHAPTER NINE

Money to burn

M ORE THAN ONE VISITOR to Dawson remarked that the wealthier miners seemed to have money to burn. That was true. Some men actually lighted cigars with fifty dollar bills. There were dozens of others who put tens of thousands of their hard earned money into a frame hotel, a saloon, or a dance hall, and then watched it reduced to ashes.

Dawson's two worst fires occurred in its climactic year. The winter of '98-'99 began and ended with blazes that destroyed, in each case, the most expensive section of town.

The first fire took place almost one year after the Thanksgiving fire of 1897. It was started by the same dance-hall girl. Half a million dollars' worth of real estate went up in smoke because Belle Mitchell set off for Louse-town leaving a candle burning in a block of wood. The fire roared up and down Front Street and back towards the hills, leaping from cabin to cabin, while two thousand men chopped up neighbouring structures to stop it from spreading.

Ironically, in front of the N.A.T. store the town's newly purchased fire-fighting equipment lay in pieces. It couldn't be used because it hadn't been paid for. Building after building, in which scores of men had flung pound after pound of gold dust, toppled and crumbled because the community wouldn't raise twelve thousand dollars for reels and hoses. Many a man had bet more than that on a single card at the faro table.

The following day a finance company hurriedly signed a note, and a fire-fighting company of one hundred men went into operation. Dawson breathed more easily. Then, in April, the newly-trained firemen asked for better wages and the town council wouldn't give it to them. The firemen struck. The fire in the boilers died. At this crucial moment, late in the night of April 26, 1899, a tongue of flame shot from the bedroom of a dance-hall girl on the second floor of the Bodega Saloon. Within minutes a holocaust began, far worse than the town had yet known.

Scores dashed to the river in the glare of the flames and tried to break through the ice to get at the water. With the boilers cold, fires had to be set to melt the frozen surface so the water could be pumped to the scene. Half of Front Street was ablaze. The temperature stood at 45° below Fahrenheit (-43°C), so cold that the heat had little effect on those standing close to the flames. Many discovered their fur coats were scorched and charred, and yet they felt nothing.

There was no breath of wind. The tongues of flame

leaped vertically into the air, causing steam to condense in an icy fog that soon covered most of the city. Within this white envelope the ghostly and frantic figures of the fire-fighters dashed about. As the dance halls and saloons began to char and totter, large barrels of liquor were overturned, and whisky ran into the streets, where it instantly froze solid in the biting cold.

The men in the river finally burned their way to the water supply. The pumps were started, and the hoses, long in disuse, slowly filled. But, as the water was ice-cold, it froze solid long before reaching the nozzles. There came a ripping, rending sound as the expanding ice tore open the hoses, followed by a moan of despair as the crowd realized the town was doomed.

"What's to be done?" cried Tom Chisholm as the flames darted towards his Aurora Saloon.

Captain Cortlandt Starnes of the Mounties supplied the answer: "Blow up the buildings in front of the fire!"

A dog team raced to the Alaska Commercial Company's warehouse for fifty pounds (22.6 kg) of giant blasting powder. Then the police wrecked the Aurora and another building to leave a blank space in front of the moving wall of flame.

By this time the whole town was involved. Thousands struggled in and out of condemned buildings carrying articles saved from the blaze, until the marsh behind the business section was littered with goods. Many were offering ten dollars an hour for help. Any two-horse team and driver could command a hundred dollars an hour. The manager of the Bank of British North America pledged a thousand dollars to anyone who could save his building. The offer was made in vain.

The town began to shudder with explosions as the dynamite did its work. Firemen, unable to pump water, worked ahead of the explosions, soaking blankets in mud puddles to try and save buildings on the edge of the blaze. At last the groaning multitude saw that further effort was useless. Half freezing, half roasting, they stood like lost souls on the edge of the Pit, their faces glowing redly in the reflected light of the flames. Front Street, with all its memories, was being consigned to the inferno.

Bill McPhee's Pioneer Saloon, one of Dawson's oldest log buildings, crumbled to ashes and was gone in a shower of sparks. The piles of gold and stacks of mail piled behind the bar were buried beneath the charred timbers

"Gather up the money, the town is going to go!" some called as McPhee made a final dash into his building.

But this was not what he was after.

"To hell with the money!" he shouted. "I want to save my moose-head," and back he staggered with his prize trophy. It meant far more to him than fleeting gold, for it had hung above the bar since opening day – that day which seemed so long ago, when Dawson was young, and the newcomers had hardly arrived and his old friends were still alive. Could it have been only two years past?

Harry Ash's Northern Saloon went the way of the Pioneer. Across the street the Aurora was blown to bits to make a firebreak. Now the Tivoli Theatre was crumbling and the Opera House, and the Dominion Saloon and Gambling House where the stakes were so high that eight Mounties sometimes had to be posted to keep order.

Walter Washburn, a faro-dealer who had invested ten thousand dollars in the Opera House, watched quietly as it was devoured by the flames. "Well," he said, "that's the way I made it, and that's the way it's gone, so what the hell!"

At this moment the vault in the tottering Bank of British North America burst wide open in the fierce heat and the contents spewed out onto the debris – gold dust and

In the spring of 1899 a terrible fire swept through Dawson, destroying more than one hundred buildings.

nuggets scooped from the bowels of Bonanza by moiling men, heavy gold watches, from the vests of gamblers and saloon-keepers, left for safe-keeping, jewelled stickpins and bracelets and dance-hall girls' diamonds, bought with favours and with wine and with music, and now fused into the molten mass that oozed from the shattered strong box to mingle with the steaming clay.

One hundred and seventeen buildings were destroyed that night. The loss was reckoned at more than one million dollars. The next day the townspeople crept from their

homes to view the havoc. The fire had died away, leaving a smoking ruin where the business section had been. On the north edge of this black scar was the Monte Carlo, scorched, but still standing. On the south the Fairview Hotel presented a grotesque sight, completely sheathed in frozen mud. In its lobby, scores of exhausted homeless men and women were sleeping in two-hour shifts.

The river marked the western boundary of the fire, the littered swamp the eastern. In the heart of the city was an enormous gap, from the ashes of which a large number of shapeless sawdust-covered piles rose at scattered intervals. These were immense blocks of ice which had been cut from the river for summertime use and covered with sawdust as insulation. Of all things, they alone had survived the fearful heat.

At once the town began to rebuild. Within twelve hours after his saloon was lost, Tom Chisholm had erected a big tent labelled "Aurora" and was doing business again. And once again the familiar sound of saw and hammer was quickly heard on Front Street.

The town that rose from the ashes was a newer and sturdier metropolis. Sewers were installed, the roads paved, new sidewalks built. The shops were full of fancy goods displayed behind plate-glass windows. Schools were going up. Scores of handsome women sauntered up and down in fashions imported from Paris.

When the river broke, more and more steamboats lined the river bank – as many as eleven at a time. Already the trip from St. Michael had been cut from twenty-one to sixteen days. Dawson was no longer a camp of tents and log cabins. Dressed lumber and plate glass were replacing bark and canvas.

The dog had had his day. Horses now moved easily through the dry streets drawing huge dray wagons. Houses had parlours, parlours had pianos, pianos stood on carpeted floors. Men began to wear white shirts, polish their boots, shave their beards, and trim their moustaches.

Dawson was no longer the isolated community it had once been. In March one man actually bicycled all the way to Skagway without mishap in a mere eight days. The White Pass Railway from Skagway to the head of the Yukon River was swiftly becoming a reality. Before the year was out, men would be riding in style where two seasons before horses had perished by the thousands.

Now the old-timers began to get an uneasy sensation in their spines. It was as if the whole cycle of their experience was being repeated. That feeling was communicated to the newcomers, who were already thinking of themselves as old-timers. Some had spent the winter in hastily built cabins in distant valleys, sinking shafts on barren claims, far from the golden axis of Bonanza and Eldorado Creeks. Many had gone to work as labourers for fifteen dollars a day or as clerks in stores or as bartenders. And some had done nothing but sit in their cabins, slowly consuming their thousand pounds of food and wondering what to do.

A sense of anti-climax spread among all of them. Thousands walked the wooden sidewalks seeking work; but there was less and less work to be had. A stale taste began to grow in the mouths of these same men who, a year before, had tumbled in confusion from the boats with shouts of triumph and anticipation.

In the outside world, the word "Klondike," which had once inspired visions of fortune, had become an expression of contempt and derision. The newest expression of disgust was the phrase, "Ah – go to the Klondike!" In Seattle goldpans had been converted to dishpans and were selling at bargain rates.

All through the spring vague rumours of something exciting on Norton Sound near the mouth of the Yukon River had been filtering into Dawson. At first the news was sketchy, as it always was, and people refused to believe it, as they always did. But skeptical or not, they began to trickle out of town and down the river in twos and threes, and then in dozens, and then in scores, searching not so much for new adventure and new wealth perhaps, but simply for the love of the search.

By mid-summer, 1899, the news from the beaches of Alaska was confirmed. On the sands of Nome, just across the Bering Strait from Siberia, a fortune in fine gold dust had been discovered – a fortune that had been lying hidden all the time at the far end of the golden river, on whose cold breast so many men had floated in a search for treasure.

The news roared across Alaska and across the Yukon Territory like a forest fire. A tent city was springing up on the beach at Nome; men were making fortunes and losing them just as quickly; buildings were going up, saloons opening, money changing hands. The beach was staked for thirteen miles (21 km); and the experts were already predicting that the new find would produce two million dollars in the first year alone – more than the Klondike had at the same time in history.

The story was beginning again, like a continuous film show at a movie house. In Dawson, log cabins could be had for the taking as steamboat after steamboat, jammed from steerage to upper deck, puffed out of the town en route to Nome. The saloon trade fell off; real estate dropped; dance halls lost their customers; Arizona Charlie Meadows announced he would float his Palace Grand in one piece down the river to the new strike.

In a single week in August eight thousand people left Dawson forever. The gaudy gold rush year was over and the City of Gold began its long decline.

When the author of this book was born, in 1920, Dawson's total population was not much more than one thousand people. Today, with the price of gold going higher, the permanent population has increased to fifteen hundred. Many of the old buildings have been restored for the tourist trade, and these include the oldest dance hall of all. Arizona Charlie didn't make good his plan to float his boat down the river. The Palace Grand Dance Hall can be seen today in Dawson, much as it was in the days of 1898 – a symbol of a bygone time, when men believed that a fortune in gold would buy anything. They learned the hard way that it wasn't the gold that counted, but rather the adventure of searching for it.

Index

Coming Soon

DR. KANE OF
THE ARCTIC SEAS

Slender, sickly, snobbish, Dr. Elisha Kent Kane was a most unlikely explorer of Canada's forbidding frozen North. But after this handsome physician died of a stroke in 1857, he was hailed as "America's greatest explorer."

In *Dr. Kane of the Arctic Seas,* Pierre Berton looks at the man behind the myth and captures both the heroism and the folly of Kane's attempts to find the so-called "Open Polar Sea" – a vast "lake" of still, ice-free water that some imagined was rather like the Mediterranean Sea!